FIVE KIN

BY SHELAGH STEPHENSON

★

★

DRAMATISTS
PLAY SERVICE
INC.

FIVE KINDS OF SILENCE
Copyright © 2004, Shelagh Stephenson

All Rights Reserved

FIVE KINDS OF SILENCE was originally produced by Out of the Blue Productions at the Lyric Hammersmith Theatre in London, England, opening on May 31, 2000. It was directed by Ian Brown; the set design was by Peter McKintosh; the lighting design was by Hugh Vanstone; and the original music was by Barrington Pheloung. The cast was as follows:

BILLY .... Tim Piggot-Smith
SUSAN .... Gina McKee
JANET .... Lizzy McInnerny
MARY .... Linda Basset
POLICEMAN, DETECTIVE,
PSYCHIATRIST, LAWYER .... Gary Whitaker
POLICE INSPECTOR,
PSYCHIATRIST, LAWYER .... Dione Inman

CHARACTERS

BILLY

SUSAN

JANET

MARY

POLICEMAN/DETECTIVE/PSYCHIATRIST/LAWYER

POLICE INSPECTOR/PSYCHIATRIST/LAWYER

FIVE KINDS OF SILENCE

Music.

BILLY. One night, I dreamt I was a dog. The moon was out, I could smell it. Ice-white metal smell. I could smell the paving stones, wet, sharp. The tarmac road made my dog teeth tingle, it was aniseed, rubber, and then the lampposts, studded with smells they were. Studded with jewels of wood metal meat. And the stars pierced my dog nose like silver wires. A woman came out of her house, sickly the smell of her, rotten, she smelt of armpits and babies and fish and a hundred other things screaming at me like a brass band. I knew what she'd had for her tea. I knew she was pregnant. I could smell it. She didn't look at me, just walked straight on by, thought I was just a dog. I laughed a quiet dog laugh: you think I'm a dog but I'm Billy, I'm me. The night smells of soot and frost and petrol and beer. I'm at my own door now. I don't need to see it, it comes to meet me, a cacophony, the smells are dancing towards me, the smells of home. I'm inside the house now. Hot citrus smell of electric light. My wife, my daughters, stand up as I come into the room. Oh, home, the smells I love, all the tiny shimmering background smells, and the two I love the most, the two smells that fill the room like a siren. One of them is fear: burning tyres, vinegar, piss. And the other one, is the smell of blood, matted in Mary's hair. I gave her a good kicking before I went out. *(Blackout. A TV cartoon programme tinkles. A shot rings out. Lights up: Billy is sprawled on his back on a single bed. Janet, Susan and his wife Mary stand around him. Susan is holding a rifle.)*
JANET. Is he dead?
SUSAN. He's stopped moving, Janet. *(Mary comes in, bewildered.)*
JANET. I'm frightened he's not dead.

MARY. What've you done Susan?

SUSAN. We had to kill him, Mum.

MARY. Is he dead? You shouldn't have done it. *(Pause.)* I should have done it.

JANET. He's moving. I can see him moving.

SUSAN. He's dead.

JANET. Give me the gun. Best be sure. *(Susan reloads the rifle and hands it to Janet.)*

MARY. Give it to me. I should do it.

JANET. No. No Mum. *(She fires at his chest. He bucks and subsides. They all stare at him fearful that he might suddenly revive. Dead Billy's voice comes out of nowhere. They don't hear it as they watch his body for signs of life.)*

BILLY. *(V.O.)* No need to do it twice. I was dead the first time. Like shooting a dog in its kennel. They got me when I was down, see. I didn't stand a chance. Bitches. It wasn't a fair fight.

JANET. We should have done it years ago.

MARY. I'll call the police then, shall I?

SUSAN. We need a drink.

JANET. We'll drink his whisky. We'll drink all of it.

MARY. Later we'll get the police. *(Susan gets whisky.)* He looks nice like that. Lying there nice and still. In his red shirt.

SUSAN. It's blood. The shirt was white.

MARY. Still, he looks nice and neat. Nice and tidy. He'd be pleased. He never liked mess.

JANET. Why doesn't he close his eyes?

MARY. D'you think he looks a bit surprised? *(Susan hands out whisky.)*

SUSAN. Drink. *(They gulp it down in silence, the TV still tinkling in the background.)*

JANET. Susan?

SUSAN. What?

JANET. Is his eye flickering? Can you see it?

SUSAN. He's dead.

JANET. Look. There, there.

SUSAN. We killed him. We had to do it. Nothing's flickering.

JANET. If he comes back to life I'll top myself. *(Fade down lights on women. Bring up light on Billy, still in his blood-stained shirt.)*

BILLY. Wet sheets, steam, cold slapping against my face, I'm hiding. Suddenly someone's here. Big white arms. Big bony hands that do things I don't like. Punch me. Other stuff. What? What other stuff? She's big, huge. Veins in her white legs, like blue knotted ropes. Rotten cheese. Ugly, I hate looking at them. Muscles at the back of the knees, bulging, yellow skin on the heels. Clatter of what? Clogs on a hard floor. Noise that splits my head in two, hot metally taste in my mouth. Crack goes the bone of my head. Stars float, I'm laughing, ha ha, hit me again if you want, I won't cry. I never cry, me. Crack, I slip in the wet. Crack goes another bone, elbow maybe. The side of my head burns. Out of my mouth comes a noise like kittens make when you drown them. But no, I'm laughing, that's what I'm doing, I don't care me, if you cut off my arms and legs, if you hit me with the belt till my skin peels off I won't cry. I'd just laugh, right. But when I get bigger I'll bloody kill you. *(Crossfade to the women, with a police officer. Billy walks over to join them.)*

MARY. Can I get you a cup of tea, Officer?

SUSAN. We did it. My sister and I did it. Mum was in the other room.

MARY. I was there.

JANET. No, she wasn't. We did it.

POLICEMAN. You two shot your father?

JANET. Is he dead?

POLICEMAN. They're taking him away now.

SUSAN. But is he dead?

JANET. We shot him twice. Was that enough?

SUSAN. Will we go to prison?

POLICEMAN. Was it an accident?

JANET. We don't mind if we go to prison. Do we Susan?

SUSAN. We don't mind. No.

MARY. If you could just tell us if he's dead, Officer.

POLICEMAN. It seems that way.

SUSAN. Are you sure?

POLICEMAN. I'm not qualified to say.

JANET. I told you, I saw his eye flickering.

POLICEMAN. Was there a reason for shooting him? You must have had a reason.

ALL. We don't want to talk about that.

MARY. If you don't mind.

POLICEMAN. Something's gone on hasn't it?

MARY. Things have been … quite tense recently.

SUSAN. Tense, yes.

JANET. What with his fits.

MARY. Six a day sometimes.

SUSAN. Our nerves have been bad.

MARY. Never knew when a fit would take him.

POLICEMAN. He was having fits so you shot him? Is that what you're saying?

MARY. He wasn't … he wasn't an easy man.

SUSAN. He was a difficult man.

POLICEMAN. And that's your reason is it? *(Silence.)* Is it?

JANET. We don't want to talk about it. If you don't mind. *(Music. Fade down lights. Lights up on Billy. Janet is sitting quietly in dimmer lighting, with a policewoman who is taking down details.)*

BILLY. I'm in bed, it's pitch dark, I'm holding my knees up to my chest. Icy, icy cold, you can't sleep for it, not even with your coat on and your boots. There's shouting along the landing, banging, same as every night, he's drunk. She's screaming at him: You bastard you useless bloody bastard, you're no bloody good to me, and he's roaring like a bull in an abattoir, no words, too drunk for that. Under the covers now, me, stop it stop it but I can hear them, I know them. I've seen them biting and tearing and heads banged off walls teeth fly blood spurts. You stupid drunk pig! They're staggering, three steps this way, three steps that, one two three, one two three. Wood splinters. You stupid drunk blind fuck pig! I hear them fall, feel his bones, his blind head hits each stair, sinews tear and snap. She says get out, you're no good to anyone. I'm out of bed now, running downstairs. The front door's open, she's trying to throw him into the street but she's holding him round the throat and she screams like this arrgghh, like a banshee. I don't want my mother to make noises like that so I kick her, I don't know why, but I do. He's on his hands and knees in the street, there's frost on the ground, glittering. He gets up and falls over because he's drunk and he's blind, and his hands are stretched out, he wants someone to help him. Sounds come from him, there's

8

snot and tears. Bitch, he says, bitch. Stupid blind bastard, stop it, stop crying Dad, you mustn't ever cry, I don't like looking at you when you do that, I don't like hearing you. I'm glad when she slams the door. She punches my head, bang, what are you doing up? It's cold upstairs, Mum, it's pitch black dark, it's like being blind I don't want to go blind like my dad I don't want to go blind. She pulls me by my arm, twists with both hands like she's wringing out washing. Don't be so bloody soft, don't be so bloody soft. I don't like to think about him out there in the dark, banging into things. I don't like to think about it. So I don't. *(Crossfade lights to Janet and policeman.)*

JANET. Is this a cell?

POLICEMAN. Yes.

JANET. It's beautiful.

POLICEMAN. You should try and get some sleep now.

JANET. I could live here.

POLICEMAN. I'll take your belt.

JANET. You're not to lock the door.

POLICEMAN. I know.

JANET. I'm on anti-depressants.

POLICEMAN. I know.

JANET. I've never slept on my own.

POLICEMAN. How old are you Janet?

JANET. Thirty-four. I've always slept with my sister.

POLICEMAN. Even when you went on holiday.

JANET. We've never been on holiday. We've never been anywhere.

POLICEMAN. The door will be open. I'll be right outside.

JANET. We had to do it you know.

POLICEMAN. I'll be right outside.

JANET. You don't know what it's been like. Your life's normal. We come from a different world. *(Crossfade to Mary and a police inspector [female] on the other side of the room.)*

MARY. I walked into the room, I picked up the gun and I shot him.

INSPECTOR. We know you didn't Mary. Your prints aren't on the weapon.

MARY. Pardon?

INSPECTOR. The fingerprints aren't yours. We know the girls did it. They told us. *(A beat.)*

MARY. Oh.

INSPECTOR. Why?

MARY. Why what?

INSPECTOR. Why did they shoot their father? *(Pause.)*

MARY. I think something ... burst ... *(Crossfade to Susan talking to male detective.)*

DETECTIVE. I'm just trying to imagine what led you to do it, Susan.

SUSAN. It was fitting. We shot him.

DETECTIVE. What did he do to you?

SUSAN. Nothing.

DETECTIVE. How old are you Susan?

SUSAN. Thirty-six.

DETECTIVE. Ever had a boyfriend?

SUSAN. No.

DETECTIVE. What about your sister?

SUSAN. No.

DETECTIVE. Never?

SUSAN. We were very close as a family. We didn't need that sort of thing.

DETECTIVE. Most girls have boyfriends at some time in their lives. Why not you?

SUSAN. We ... had each other.

DETECTIVE. Did he knock you about? *(Pause.)*

SUSAN. Sometimes ...

DETECTIVE. Your mother? Your sister?

SUSAN. Sometimes.

DETECTIVE. Badly?

SUSAN. He had ... quite a temper. Sometimes.

DETECTIVE. What got him in a temper? *(Pause.)*

SUSAN. Things.

DETECTIVE. Such as? *(Pause.)*

SUSAN. We weren't to make a noise when we clicked on the light switch. Plates clattering. That wasn't allowed. *(Pause.)* Sometimes we buttered his toast wrong.

DETECTIVE. Sometimes you buttered his toast wrong?

SUSAN. In the wrong direction. The butter in the wrong direction.

DETECTIVE. I see ...

SUSAN. No you don't. How could you see? You couldn't begin.

DETECTIVE. Tell me then. Explain. Then maybe I will see.

SUSAN. I'm tired. I'm very tired. Don't ask me anything else, I just want to sleep now. I just want to sleep for a very long time. I think I'm coming down with something.

DETECTIVE. You haven't told me everything Susan.

SUSAN. I'm sorry. I'm tired. I'm not well. *(Pause.)*

DETECTIVE. Did he sleep with you? *(Billy walks into the room.)*

SUSAN. What? I think I've got a temperature. I'm burning. My face is burning. Is the room tilting?

DETECTIVE. Did he do anything sexual to you?

SUSAN. I'm sorry, you must think I'm drunk. Is it me or is it the room skewed like this? My head's in flames. I need aspirins. I need a doctor. I'm coming down with something

DETECTIVE. Your sister's told us he did. She told us he slept with both of you.

SUSAN. Oh. Oh. *(Billy stands at her shoulder now.)*

BILLY. Gather your thoughts, say nothing, take your time, there's still time. Don't say a word unless it's no. Laugh at him, go on. Laugh. She's a bloody liar that Janet. Tell him she's mental.

SUSAN. I've dry mouth.

DETECTIVE. He did, didn't he? Since you were thirteen years old. *(Silence. Susan speaks in a quiet, cracked voice.)*

SUSAN. Yes.

BILLY. You bloody bitch, you've done it now. You said the thing that should never be said.

DETECTIVE. Can I get you a drink of water?

BILLY. Snatch the yes back, take it back, go on. Shout no, no, I didn't mean that —

SUSAN. I —

DETECTIVE. I'll fetch you some water.

BILLY. You're opening your mouth, go on, speak —

SUSAN. I —

BILLY. There's rubble in your throat, ignore it. Just shout no you stupid bitch, don't listen to the things crashing in your head —

SUSAN. I'm very sorry — *(She gets up and her legs give way.)*

BILLY. And now a rush of fear unties your bladder. They've tricked you Susan, I'm not dead, not dead at all, and soon I'll burst through the window and kill you. Water streaming down her leg. Her eyes streaming. The dam is breached, the walls have collapsed. Get up off the floor you stupid bitch. Get up off the floor. *(Crossfade to Mary and female Inspector.)*

INSPECTOR. I need some help here Mary. I'm in the dark. Can you tell me a little about yourself maybe?

MARY. There's nothing to tell.

INSPECTOR. I'll fetch you a cup of tea. Would that help?

MARY. That'd be nice. Thank you. *(The inspector goes out.)* I'm six years old, walking home from school. There's deep snow crunching on the ground and my feet are tingling cold. I have on Wellingtons and green woollen mittens threaded through my sleeves with elastic. I get to my street, and before I can get to our house Auntie Ruby comes out of it in a black fur hat, and hurries me away. Oh the mite she says, oh the mite. In my head it muddles with Almighty God whose Son suffered and died because He loved us. Imagine the nails Mary. Imagine the nails, Sister Bridget says, being driven into Our Lord's beautiful hands. Think of the pain, Mary, think of the blood, as the nail is driven through sinew and bone and soft, soft flesh. He suffered this because He loved us so much. I'm thinking this all the way to Auntie Ruby's. I'm thinking let the dark thing not happen, I will dwell upon the suffering of Our Lord, I will drive nails into my own hands only let it not happen. Ruby's house is dark and cold and something terrible is wrong, the praying didn't work. My food congeals on the plate, my heart lodged in my throat like a stone. Why can't I go home, but I know the world has ended. Your poor mother. Your poor mother, is what they say. That chop will be put in front of you at every meal until you eat it. But my throat is closed. I will never eat again. Days pass, there are carols on the wireless, I feed the chop to the dog and my mother is not coming back. They've put her in the ground, they say. But won't she be cold? How will she breathe? How will she eat? Won't she be lonely? It is Christmas, and my poor mother is deep in the ground, up by the moor. I go back to my home. No point lighting a fire says my father. We won't be having a tree. On Christmas Day I sit hunched in my coat, longing for my mother to come up out of the lonely cold ground, watching my father drink a bottle of whisky. I am mad with grief he says, forgive me. I don't know what grief is but I start to cry anyway. I cry louder and louder but my mother never comes and my father doesn't wake. Through the wall, I can hear the neighbours having a sing-song. *(The inspector returns with a polystyrene cup of tea.)*

INSPECTOR. Ready to tell me anything?

MARY. It was him or us. He was going down and he was taking us with him. We were frightened. We thought one day he'll kill us all and then shoot himself. And no one will ever know what went on. It's form of torture to think that no one will ever know, isn't it? *(Crossfade to Susan and Janet talking together.)*

SUSAN and JANET. *(Together.)* Dear Mum, we are in a lovely place with gardens and a small pond with fish, and it is beautiful here. Last night we had baths with as much water as we wanted and it was as close to heaven as we've ever been. Everyone is kind, and our rooms are warm, people say the rules are strict but we just laugh, Janet and me. Sometimes we talk to lawyers. They are very nice. This is the first time we've been free in the whole of our lives which is funny really when you think about it because a remand centre is actually a sort of prison isn't it? Your loving daughters Susan and Janet. *(Crossfade to Mary with male psychiatrist.)*

PSYCHIATRIST. Are you sleeping now Mary?

MARY. In the night he comes back to accuse me. He says you let them kill me, now I'll have to kill you.

PSYCHIATRIST. He can't harm you anymore.

MARY. I love you he said. Practically straightaway. I believed him. I was twenty. I knew nothing. I was lonely and he was handsome. And now he'll never leave. It'll never be over, it'll never end. Every time I look in the mirror, he's there. Scars. That was the time he did this or that, here is where he broke my fingers. When he comes into my dreams I think my heart will stop. That's how he'll kill me. I'll die of fright. *(Crossfade to Janet with female lawyer. Dialogue between * and * overlaps.)*

LAWYER. * We're trying to prepare a case for the defence —

JANET. I had clinical depression. That's what they called it. The doctors kept saying why Janet, why are you like this?

LAWYER. — so if you can tell us everything you can about what happened —

JANET. Every morning, wake up crying. It made him mad, he wanted me to smile, go on, take that look of yours, smile Janet, smile, or people might catch on —

LAWYER. — I think we may be able to provide a very strong case —

JANET. I couldn't do it anymore, the muscles in my face stopped functioning.

LAWYER. — for citing mitigation, over a period of years —

JANET. He'd shout you lot've got everything, you want for nothing.

LAWYER. Perhaps you'd like a cup of tea — *

JANET. Every time I went to the hospital, is there anything you want to tell us? No, nothing, no. Because what could I say? Where would I start? And if I did, I knew he'd kill us all. Mum, then Susan, then me. In that order. Then himself. I knew he would because he told me.

LAWYER. What did you feel when you'd shot him?

JANET. Pardon me?

LAWYER. When you shot him, what were your feelings?

JANET. What did you feel here, what did you feel there? Where did the intercourse take place? What difference does it make? The pictures in my head are mine, and giving them to you won't wipe them out —

LAWYER. Janet? Are you listening?

JANET. I felt nothing.

LAWYER. Did you feel relieved, elated?

JANET. You think he's gone now he's dead. But the dead don't go anywhere, they dance in your head, they come to you at night. The dead don't die, I know that now.

LAWYER. Did you love him?

JANET. Of course we did. He was our father. *(Crossfade to Billy.)*

BILLY. I don't remember pain, I don't remember pleasure. I was born aged six with teeth and a black, black heart. I'm what, eight? She has a new man now, a soft milky thing, no match for my lost blind dad. He winds wool for her with his limp fish hands. A voice like gruel. Boneless he is. And yet. And yet … dark feet like blocks of ice, heart bumping against my throat. Voices burbling in the blackness, "Is anybody there? Is anybody there?" They got a drowned man once, he spoke with weeds tangled in his throat, I heard him. He opens his mouth and it's not his voice come out it's dead people. Not frightened, me, I'm just cold, that's what that

14

banging noise is in my chest, cramp in my leg. Dry tongue. Stupid bastards don't know I'm here. Stupid bastards. There's someone coming through, he says, there's someone coming through, it's Mam. Stupid bastards, I don't believe them I wish someone would put the light on the skin's going tight on the top of my head I think I'm having a heart attack — MAM! Billy? Is that you? Let me stay, I want to stay I won't make no noise. I told you bloody bugger, I told you. She's pulling me, dragging me upstairs, I'm fighting back, bloody get off me, bloody get off. No don't shut me up in the dark, it's black in there the black gets in my nose and mouth and eyes, I can't breathe. She says get in the cupboard, you'll have no light, you don't deserve it. Bloody bugger bastard I shout, bloody damn bugger. Crack. She hits me. Crack. Keep your fury Billy she says, you'll need it out there, but never cry, or I'll send the devil to you. No, no, I won't cry, don't send him, I don't want to see him, don't shut the door, what if he comes Mam, what if he comes? But she slams the door anyway. I won't cry, I shout, I bloody won't. Bastards … bloody damn blast shit bastards … don't send the devil to me, I don't want to see him … bloody bugger pig devil, I bloody am not I bloody am not I bloody am not frightened you buggers … you pig buggers. *(Fade to Susan talking to female Psychiatrist.)*

PSYCHIATRIST. You must feel very angry Susan.

SUSAN. Pardon me?

PSYCHIATRIST. With your mother. She let it happen all those years.

SUSAN. They said we could go home now. They said unconditional bail.

PSYCHIATRIST. Your mother was there all the time, and she did nothing to stop it did she?

SUSAN. We don't think of it like that.

PSYCHIATRIST. Why?

SUSAN. Why what?

PSYCHIATRIST. Do you sometimes feel resentful towards her perhaps?

SUSAN. Why?

PSYCHIATRIST. Why d'you think?

SUSAN. We love her. She's our mother. Why d'you want us to be angry?

PSYCHIATRIST. I wonder if sometimes you deny what you feel. I think it's understandable.

SUSAN. I think we live on different planets. *(Pause.)* I'm sorry, that was rude.

PSYCHIATRIST. You must be rude if that's how you feel.

SUSAN. Most of what you say we don't understand.

PSYCHIATRIST. You said yesterday you didn't mind going to prison. Did you mean that?

SUSAN. We killed him. He's dead. We feel better now. There's nothing you can do about any of it.

PSYCHIATRIST. Let us try. *(A beat.)*

SUSAN. This getting angry, this feeling this and feeling that. It's not for us. It's not really our sort of thing. It's too late now. You think you can understand it but you can't see the size of it. If you had to live inside our heads for five minutes you'd go mad and die. Best we deal with it ourselves. *(Crossfade to Billy.)*

BILLY. Our town is full of soldiers. There's a war on. I like the shine on their boots, I like the sound they make on the cobbles, harsh and strong, it sets my teeth tingling. They are polished and trim and neat these men, belted and tucked and ready for action. Already I'm hooked. I follow them to their barracks, oh the neatness of it, the rows of bunks, the order, I'm beside myself with longing. Each bed tight made, corners neat and parcelled, no gaps, no mistakes, there's method in this. The air smells of carbolic and boot polish and engine grease. One of them shows me his kit, his boots gleaming under his bunk, placed just so, at just such an angle, the precision of it makes me feel faint and then a quivery ripple shivers across my groin. I am at home here. I am in paradise here. They take me to show me the storerooms. Miles of shelving, stacked to the roof with supplies. I say the word under my breath. Supplies. In case of. In the event of. Supplies. This is organisation. Nothing can go wrong here. Everything, every last thing labelled, everything in its place. The soldier talks to me in his strange accent, London or Scotland or somewhere, says you have to be organised see, because if anything's out of place, if ever there's an emergency, think of the chaos then. He shows me the order books, the requisition pads, cancellation forms, goods in, goods out, pink for in green for out and things are dancing inside my head; I'm practically singing. He lets me hold his gun. I imagine shooting all the people in our street, pop, pop, pop. I shoot them because they shouldn't be in here, messing everything up, throwing the system into disarray. I imagine the look on their faces, stupid, caught by surprise. Pop. Astonishment, pain, fear, twisted mouths, some of them even cry. I am laughing, shivers run up and down my spine, my feet are going like Fred Astaire. I feel the most pleasure I've ever felt. I think, there, there. See what it feels like. The soldier takes the gun. There's no bullets in it anyway. *(Crossfade to Mary and male psychiatrist.)*

PSYCHIATRIST. You could have left him.

MARY. I did once. I went to my father's. Took the girls and ran. My father said: you made your bed. Now lie in it. Marriage is a sacrament. Marriage is for life.

PSYCHIATRIST. Tell me about your father.

MARY. I remember this time I made supper for him, a struggle, heaving boiling kettles as big as myself, setting out the glass milk jug, just so, standing on a chair to slice bread. Baked beans it was. The battle with the tin, burning my fingers on the stove. And then the waiting. Look how good I have been, look Dad, look. Midnight he comes in and sweeps my beautiful gift from the table, crockery shattering, beans splattering against the walls. It's cold is all he says, and my heart shrivels. Later, he wakes me, and says I'm sorry Mary, forgive me, and that one thing makes me leap for joy inside, because it means he loves me. Doesn't it?

PSYCHIATRIST. Did Billy ever say, "I'm sorry, Mary"?

MARY. At the beginning. Yes. Then after, nothing. I longed for him to say it, but he never did. When he came to get me from my dad's that time, he gave me a kiss and said, "I'm sorry, let's make up." And there was a bit of the old Billy there, the one I loved. I wanted to believe him and so I went home. When we got in the door he broke my ribs. Jumped on them. I never went again. He said if I did he'd find us and kill us.

PSYCHIATRIST. You mentioned "the old Billy." What does that mean?

MARY. When I met him he was gentle. Walked me to my door. Said you're the one for me. Said he'd known straightaway. I wish I had a lad like that they all said. Polite and quiet and handsome. His mother said: If you marry our Billy, he'll put you through the eye of a needle. I didn't know what she meant. I do now. I was soft and shy, not the sort to argue. I was lonely. I was a bit of a wallflower. He must have seen me coming. *(Fade to Billy. Band music plays.)*

BILLY. Tarts. Primping and powdering and giving you the eye, wouldn't mind if they meant it but no, half the time they'd hardly give you a feel, not that I'd want one. Not that I'd want one. Other fish to fry, me. They don't know, see. They can't see the rays coming off me. No idea, any of them. I'd wipe the smiles off their faces, I'd knock their bloody blocks off, I'd have them on their knees begging, they'd be. On their backs, begging. I'm tanked up, a bursting thing. I can feel the blood pounding in my head. I'm thinking how when I get like this I do things. Dark, jittery things. I'm thinking how I killed next door's cat to see how it felt. Better, I felt better for a while, seeing it squirm and cry, it was better than feeling up one of those tarts. There's a look I like to see, fear is it, face twists, mouth pleads. I fizz and burn, my insides leap. Then after, nothing, dead is what I feel. It reminds me of something. I can't remember what. I'm just thinking this when I see her. Sitting quiet like a rabbit, none of the lipstick, none of the flash. She looks up at me. I know I'll marry her. This is the woman. This is the woman. This is the one. I see my life mapped out before me, I see her, I see children, I see a world. In a flash it comes together. I'm a pioneer. I'm in enemy territory, I'm going to knock it into shape, impose a bit of order. I dance in my heart. The world is black and cold but I'm taking her with me. She smiles. I feel like I did in the army barracks. It's better than killing the cat. Although somehow, that's muddled in with it too. *(Crossfade to Janet. Billy comes and stands behind her as she speaks.)*

JANET. I can't sleep Mum, I can't sleep on my own the bed's too big, things creak, footsteps on the stair, out in the corridor. I think it's him, every time I think it's him. They say he's dead but what if he's not? The golden glow's gone. Euphoria they said, hysteria. Small dreams I had then, a glimpse of him, a hand here, a breath there, but quick to go. He's shrinking I thought, death has shrivelled him. He's back now, the whole of him, his breath on my face, his hands in my hair, pulling me to places I want to forget. I'm not strong like Susan, soon I will die of this. Big dreams now, huge dreams. Close my eyes and I'm trapped in the film of our life. Snap. Another photo. Snap. Smile Janet, smile. What will they make of these happy family snaps, our sandals and frocks, our arms entwined, a rabbit eating grass at our feet. And we're smiling smiling smiling for our lives but at the back of my head I say please someone read this secret sign, I'm sending you a message, read it read it please. This is not real, this is not true, can't you see it in my eye. He kicks us where it can't be seen, under our hair, under our clothes, he boots us across the room. I want to tear off my dress and shout look look look look look. I look at the photo and where is the message, the sign in my eye? I look at the photo and we're just smiling. *(Fade to Mary and lawyer, near the bed.)*

LAWYER. Is this the…?

MARY. This is where he died, yes. He did look peaceful. You'd never think to look at him he'd been shot. *(The lawyer looks at the bed, trying to fathom the situation.)*

LAWYER. Why did you put up with it so long Mary?

MARY. And this is his medication list. *(She hands him a piece of paper.)*

LAWYER. Four Phenytion, two vitamin, one blood pressure —

MARY. He liked to have it down on paper. Always best to have things in writing.

LAWYER. Like what?

MARY. Oh, most things really. Rules. Lists. Because, you see if we didn't there was always a risk.

LAWYER. Of what?

MARY. That something might go wrong.

LAWYER. Why did you tolerate this? *(Mary turns away.)* D'you mind if I look upstairs?

MARY. No. Go on. *(He goes. Mary sits on the bed. Billy is in the shadows behind her.)* A flickering memory I have, of warmth and light, a wireless playing when I come home from school, but this is long ago, before they put my mother in the ground. After that, nothing. Every night come home; nobody. No fire, he even sold the wireless. It's not his fault. It's not his fault, I won't have that, he loves me, and I love him so hard my chest hurts, but there's drink and a great sadness and I'm so small I can't help. The first winter, I think it's the first, freezing fog and my heart like lead, I'm

19

waiting in the parlour for him. Waiting, and aching, like a dog, every footstep in the street, every fleeting sound, my head cocked. Is he coming? Is he coming? He never does. Long past dark he stumbles in the door with a bag of chips or a bottle of pop, I'm sorry Mary, forgive me, and he lies on the floor or the stairs or sometimes he might make the chair, and sleeps like a dead man. All those nights waiting for him, nothing stirring, just me and silence and a world going on outside. As cold and unreachable as the grave, like the place they've put my mother. Sometimes I make a mewling noise, like a cat, to see what it sounds like, to remind myself I'm still here. The noise gets louder and louder, until eventually I'm howling, howling into the darkness: come home you fucker, come home or I will howl my throat to shreds and then you'll be sorry for what you've done. He doesn't come. After a while I stop howling. No one ever comes. I think perhaps I have died, like my mother, and so I cut my arm, a big slice, with the carving knife and the pain is a good thing because it's real, a sharp true thing that skitters the stone away from my tomb. The blood flows down my arm and through my fingers, brightest flowing red. And now I know I'm not dead. The next night I do the other arm and I think of Jesus and what He suffered for love of us, and as the knife draws a ruby ribbon from shoulder to elbow I'm thinking of my father as much as the pain. I don't know why, but I am. *(She curls up on the bed. Billy comes out of the shadows.)*

BILLY. I love my family. They're mine. I love them. What's different about it, see, is that I love them more than what you might call normal. Don't ever say I don't love them because I do. I do. I've everything I want. A wife. Two girls. Glad they're girls. Nice balance. Nice sense of proportion. Me and them. Them and me. No one else. We don't need it. We don't want it. The house shipshape, it's all under control. Lay my hand on anything any time I want it. Blindfold.

MARY. When you walked into that dance hall, you handed me a port and lemon, and I recognised you, as if I'd known you all my life. I looked into your eyes and my heart welled up. Oh, I will save you, I will, I will save you —

LAWYER. *(Off.)* Mary? *(Mary gets up and goes. Billy follows her as lights come up on lawyer and shelving.)* What is all this?

MARY. It's arranged alphabetically, d'you see?

BILLY. I've got rules. I've got a system.

LAWYER. Brown polish, budgie food, bullets spare, bullets spent, curtain rings, dried peas and beans —

MARY. Pulses are in a separate section under "p."

LAWYER. Emergency supplies, fire lighters. You don't have any open fires.

BILLY. What I say goes. Trained them so they know that.

MARY. No. They were just in case.

LAWYER. Of what?

MARY. He liked to cover all eventualities. *(They walk along the shelving, the lawyer taking notes.)*

BILLY. Glasses! Five inches from edge of table.

LAWYER. Garden implements, hand cream —

BILLY. Spoons! Bowl down when you drain them —

LAWYER. Knives, macaroni —

BILLY. That blue china cat, I like that cat. Three inches from fruit bowl. Not four not two but three. What I say goes.

LAWYER. Pest poison, razor blades, rope —

BILLY. Got my eye on everything, got my ear to the ground.

MARY. Susan and Janet did the labels. They've very neat hands haven't they?

BILLY. You can't take a breath without me. Don't even try.

LAWYER. Did he ever explain the purpose of all this?

MARY. It's just spare items. Just in case.

LAWYER. Of what?

MARY. That's all he said.

BILLY. Can't take any chances, can't take any risks.

LAWYER. But didn't you ever ask?

MARY. I think he was expecting a siege.

BILLY. Got them on rations, like in the war. It's all there in writing, there's no excuse.

MARY. Or a war. An explosion of some sort. He wanted to make sure we'd survive. Just the four of us.

BILLY. Two ounces of this, one ounce of that, three of the other —

MARY. He made us do the football pools.

BILLY. Keep a little edge on their hunger, keep them on their toes —

MARY. He said if we won, he'd buy a desert island, and we'd all go and live there and never come back. That was his dream.

BILLY. I'm the one that needs feeding up. I'm the one who has to go out there. Earn a crust. In the cold, in the dark, there's all sorts of stuff.

MARY. It was our nightmare.

BILLY. You've no idea. You lot don't know you're born.

MARY. We must have been the only family in England praying not to win. *(Crossfade to Susan and female lawyer.)*

LAWYER. It's not enough Susan. You have to tell us everything. We're trying to construct a defence.

SUSAN. I've told you.

LAWYER. When did he first start having intercourse with you?

SUSAN. I can't remember. I was quite young. Sixteen.

LAWYER. Yesterday you said thirteen.

SUSAN. It was a long time ago. I can't remember.

LAWYER. Sixteen or thirteen, which?

SUSAN. I was probably younger than sixteen. I don't know. Maybe I was thirteen.

LAWYER. And how did it happen?

SUSAN. Pardon me?

LAWYER. What were the events which led up to it?

SUSAN. He just said. He just said. You know. *(Pause.)*

LAWYER. What?

SUSAN. I was in the shed. He was chopping bones. And he just. You know.

LAWYER. In the shed?

SUSAN. Pardon me?

LAWYER. It happened in the shed?

SUSAN. No. He told me in the shed.

LAWYER. Told you what?

SUSAN. He said Susan, you know I have sex with your mother, well now I want it with you too.

LAWYER. And what did you say?

SUSAN. I just … I wasn't … I didn't know what it was. I knew it was bad. *(Pause.)* Could I have a glass of water please? *(The lawyer pours water. Susan drinks.)* So I just said I don't want to Dad, I think it's wrong. And he said what he always said which is what I say goes.

LAWYER. And?

SUSAN. And what?

LAWYER. What happened then?

SUSAN. Nothing for a couple of weeks. I felt sick. I didn't what was going to happen. I didn't know what to expect. One day he sent Mum and Janet out to a jumble sale. And that's when he did it.

LAWYER. Did you tell your mother?

SUSAN. Yes.

LAWYER. And she did nothing?

SUSAN. There was nothing she could do. He's bought a gun.

LAWYER. Did it happen regularly?

SUSAN. Every Friday. Other times in between. *(Pause.)* We were trapped. Stop looking at me like that. You don't understand. There was nothing we could do. He could have done it to you. Even someone like you. It's easy. You don't fight. You don't know how to. You keep going. You survive. *(Pause.)* You think we're freaks don't you?

LAWYER. No.

SUSAN. Your mother couldn't have saved you either. You're all in it together. You're all locked up together. And you don't tell any-one … because it's … because it's private.

LAWYER. Would you like a cup of tea?

SUSAN. I'm sorry for shouting.

LAWYER. You weren't shouting.

SUSAN. I'm sorry. Can I stop now? *(Crossfade to Janet.)*

JANET. Dear Dad, I'm writing this because the psychiatrist says I should. I'm to tell you what I feel. They ask us all the time. How does this make you feel how does that, what did you feel at this time, what did you feel at that? We know how to do it now. We say what they want. We felt vulnerable, we felt frightened, we felt terrified. What I feel is embarrassed. Words words words. Useless every one. You were our father and we killed you. We're glad you're dead but sad you weren't nicer because then we wouldn't have had to shoot you. Once, when I was seven or eight, I came in and you were at the sink playing with our goldfish you'd tipped from its bowl. You were watching it flap and gasp, with a strange dreamy look in your eye. No colour in them, all black. The corners of your mouth turned up. That's how you looked after you hit Mum.

That's all I know about you. That look. I can't write this anymore. I don't understand the point. We tell them this bit and that bit, but for them it's just some horrible incidents. A case history. Sometimes I think I'll never be free of you. Sometimes I want to come into your grave and shoot you again. And again and again and again. Just to make sure. *(Crossfade to Susan and female psychiatrist.)*

SUSAN. Is there a drug you can get to stop you dreaming?

PSYCHIATRIST. Why?

SUSAN. I'd like one.

PSYCHIATRIST. What are your dreams about?

SUSAN. Stuff. Is there a drug then? Tablets or something?

PSYCHIATRIST. Dreams can be important.

SUSAN. They're not. They're just rubbish.

PSYCHIATRIST. Sometimes dreams tell us how we really feel.

SUSAN. That's not true.

PSYCHIATRIST. Tell me about them. *(Pause.)*

SUSAN. I can't.

PSYCHIATRIST. Why can't you? Do they make you feel violent? Angry?

SUSAN. No.

PSYCHIATRIST. What then?

SUSAN. I wish I'd never said it now.

PSYCHIATRIST. You'd like the dreams to stop?

SUSAN. They're killing me. I can't live with them.

PSYCHIATRIST. Try and tell me about them. *(Long pause.)*

SUSAN. I dream that … I can't say it. I'm sorry.

PSYCHIATRIST. Could you write it?

SUSAN. I can't say it. I can't write it. I can't get rid of it. I'm burning up with it.

PSYCHIATRIST. With what? *(Susan begins to cry, in a choked, reluctant way.)* If you tell me, I'll help you carry it. I won't be shocked.

SUSAN. I can never tell the worst. I can never tell.

PSYCHIATRIST. Is your father in these dreams?

SUSAN. Of course he is.

PSYCHIATRIST. And what is he doing?

SUSAN. I can't tell you …

PSYCHIATRIST. You can you know. *(Pause.)*

24

SUSAN. He's having sex with me. He's having sex with me and I'm … and I'm … *(She breaks off.)*
PSYCHIATRIST. And you're what?
SUSAN. I'm enjoying it. *(Fade down lights. Psychiatrist goes. One light on Susan.)* She said try writing it, so I'm writing it. You come into the room. I can't see your face. It's dark. I'm lying on the bed and I've no clothes on. You kiss me a lover's kiss. You put your tongue inside my mouth and you tell me that you love me. I say I love you too. That's what lovers say isn't it. I love you too. Dad. I say I love you too Dad. I can't write this. She said the dreams will fade if I write it down. She says it's normal. These feelings are normal. I say they're not my feelings they're my dreams. You touch me. I want you to. It's you and it's not you. I ask you to touch me again. And you do. I look at your face above me, and you look so sad, and I'm not your daughter I'm your lover. Except I'm lying now because I know I'm your daughter and that's what makes it so special and secret. You look so sad and I will make everything better for you. I don't want you to stop. You're the only lover I've ever had. I pull you down towards me. I wake up. I'm sick over the side of the bed. How could you do this to me Dad? How could you do this? *(Crossfade to Janet and Mary.)*
JANET. We can come home next week. Until the trial.
MARY. That's very kind of them.
JANET. We're not a danger to society.
MARY. Of course you're not. *(Susan comes in.)*
SUSAN. They've given Janet a tape.
JANET. A relaxation tape. I listen to it on a Walkman.
MARY. Does it help?
JANET. No.
SUSAN. She's not doing it right.
MARY. It'll be better when we're all back together.
JANET. I'll sleep in your bed.
MARY. Yes.
JANET. Until the dreams stop.
SUSAN. What's it like without him Mum?
MARY. I had mushrooms on toast yesterday. I haven't had that since I was a girl.
SUSAN. We went shopping yesterday. With Deidre.

JANET. She's one of the staff.
SUSAN. Very kind.
JANET. We didn't know what to buy.
SUSAN. We felt a bit lightheaded.
JANET. We felt a bit sick.
SUSAN. It was a hypermarket. We had ten pounds each.
JANET. We bought some Shredded Wheat.
SUSAN. And three packets of biscuits.
JANET. Deidre laughed. She said is that all you want?
SUSAN. But we'd never had Shredded Wheat.
JANET. We'd seen it on the telly.
SUSAN. She said you two are weird.
JANET. The weren't very nice actually. The Shredded Wheat. But I expect we'll get used to them. *(Crossfade to Billy with a rifle.)*
BILLY. The girls are grown now, I've got them taped, I've got them tabbed, don't let them out of my sight. There's men on the streets, men on the corners. I've seen them, I know what they want. Right, I say, right, no talking to men, no talking to boys, not now, not ever, d'you hear me. Point my gun, that always gets them, never argue with a gun, I taught them that. Oh yes Dad no Dad three bags full Dad, but they're bloody lying just like their mother, say one thing, mean another, don't know why they bother, I know everything. I know you, you say one word, you flash one look, we don't Dad, we don't, but they're taking the piss. *(Crossfade to Susan and Janet with social worker taking notes.)*
SUSAN. He bought us rings.
JANET. Wedding rings.
SUSAN. We went to the jeweller's and chose them ourselves.
JANET. Mine was patterned.
SUSAN. Mine was plain.
JANET. The jeweller was delighted, he said to Dad —
SUSAN. — oh, a double wedding —
JANET. — and Dad said —
BILLY. *(Joining them.)* Yes.
SUSAN. In his special voice. His outside voice.
BILLY. Yes. They'll both be wives.
JANET. And we put our rings on and left the shop.
SUSAN. He said it was to keep us safe.

JANET. To keep the men at bay.

SUSAN. And when we got home —

BILLY. You talk to men and this is what I'll do. *(He points the rifle at the audience.)* Bang, bang, bang! I fire at the wall and they jump and cower, so I do it again, I'm tingling and racing, there's holes in the wall. I fire at their feet to make them dance, oh, I'm laughing now, and then she spoils it, she bloody spoils it. She starts to cry. I've told you, I've told you, no bloody tears in this house, no bloody tears. She keeps on, she keeps on, get her out of here, get her out before the room explodes. She doesn't go. So I do, I go. I lie in the garden face down in the wet grass, gun sleeping soft beside me. Rain patters and splashes around me. I could sleep for a year. I wish I was dead. I don't know why, but I do.

SUSAN. He wasn't a bad man.

JANET. In his own way.

SUSAN. But he needed to be put down.

JANET. The way you do with dogs.

SUSAN. You put them out of their misery.

JANET. Sometimes he'd lie on the floor and shout.

BILLY. I don't want to live, I want out, I want out.

SUSAN. So really we did him a favour.

JANET. Either he went, or we all did.

SUSAN. It was just a matter of time.

JANET. He wouldn't let us leave.

SUSAN. We couldn't let him live. Sometimes he kissed us in the street, not a father's kiss. People were nearby, people we knew, and nobody said a word. No one said nothing. Janet, me, mum, dad. And no one else did either. But they knew, they saw. All that silence. Five kinds of silence. Each of ours and the world outside. Cars passed, people shopped, drinks were bought in pubs, and we slipped through it all like ghosts. This man is my father, I wanted to shout. I was banging on the glass but it made no noise, I was opening my mouth but no voice came. He was sucking away at our lives, soon we'd be gone and the dust would settle. As if we'd never been. This, most frightening of all: as if we'd never been. We felt the waters closing over us. He was dragging us down to unmourned graves, and with one last gasp, we made for the surface where we saw the light, threw ourselves on the mercy of the air. One square of light. A promise of breathing unaided, and we saw our chance in the darkness. There was no option, d'you see that? When you're drowning, you snatch at life. We came out of the dark and into the light. We are newborn babies and we are learning to walk. *(Fade down. Lights up on Billy alone. Gradually, the family appear behind him.)*

BILLY. I'm standing at the sink. Fizz, crack, there's a ripple in my head, a burning smell, my brain shattering into fragments, hundreds and thousands of coloured glass. I am dissolving. The room turns magenta pink. When I come to I'm on a bed. Epilepsy, they say. Fits. Bring me my gun I shout and no one moves a muscle. They're smiling and patting my hand. And then I realise I'm not actually talking, I'm not even moving my mouth. God damn you bastards and this last word like a roar bursts from my lungs and smashes them in the face. Oh, they can hear me now all right. Let's get this place shipshape, I'm not out for the count yet —

MARY. No Billy, the doctor says —

BILLY. Sod the bloody doctor I hope he rots in hell, bring me my gun. Crack. A noise.

MARY. Billy?

BILLY. Where did that come from? Is it outside or in my head? I say nothing. I don't let on.

MARY. Billy? D'you think he can hear me?

BILLY. Bring the gun let's have a party I'm feeling on top of the world. Tell Janet to stop crying, tell her to shut her bloody face. Let's all have a whisky, let's get this show on the road. Crack. Someone's popping something in my head. What's wrong with you lot, what are you gawping at?

MARY. You've had a fit Billy, calm down.

BILLY. She says I've had a fit, but she's just saying it. What I think is some bastard spiked my drink.

SUSAN. The fits got worse.

JANET. They took him to hospital.

MARY. And that was the happiest time of our lives.

JANET. It was lovely waking up in the morning knowing he wasn't there.

SUSAN. We could eat what we wanted.

MARY. Read magazines.

28

JANET. That's when we knew. We got a taste of forbidden fruit.

SUSAN. We understood what we didn't have. He was sunk from then on, really.

MARY. When he first came home he seemed different.

JANET. Weak as a kitten. Quiet as a lamb.

SUSAN. We were walking on air.

MARY. But it didn't last.

JANET. That last weekend was like being in hell. *(The television comes on, a tinkling cartoon programme.)*

BILLY. Another little whisky. Everything's under control. More crackling in my head last night, I didn't say a word. Give them an inch and they'll take a mile. A bird in the hand is worth two in the bush. What I say goes, what I say goes. Somebody come up here, I'm on my own in the dark. Mary Susan Janet somebody come and do something. Stop bloody crying Janet you live the life of Riley, you don't want for nothing. Any more tears and I'll break your neck. Another little whisky. Crack. Sparks fly. Bright phosphorescence. My brain hisses and fizzes. Crack. Oh. Oh. I am hurtling through black sky on a sea of pungent scent. I can smell the colours of my own mind, I can smell this television programme, I'm back to my dog self, back to the dream. Metal, I smell metal and wood and cordite — *(Susan picks up the gun.)* Janet's tears, Susan's breasts, I smell something blinding white and relentless. I smell things I can't control. Piss, my piss, something between my teeth —

SUSAN. Bite on this Dad, bite on this —

JANET. I can't go on, load the gun —

BILLY. Oh burning tyres, spent diesel, an overtone of brass, stinging nettles, cold sweat, I love that smell so why don't I love it now. My body bucking, the room is rank with it, my eyes stream with it, my fear is filling the room. Bang. Bang. Bang. *(Fade down lights on Billy. Mary, Janet and Susan walk into the light.)*

MARY. Let it end here. Let it end with us. I don't want grandchildren. Let the blight end here.

SUSAN and JANET. *(Together.)* When the judge told us we weren't going to prison, we wanted to say thank you but nothing came out. She said you've suffered enough. That was very kind of her we thought.

SUSAN. We can start a new life now.
JANET. We've got a maisonette.
MARY. We plan to have pink carpets.
SUSAN. And a dog.
JANET. We've got four bedrooms.
MARY. One for each of us.
SUSAN. And one for spare items.
JANET. We've already bought the shelving. *(Music. Fade down lights.)*

End of Play

PROPERTY LIST

Rifle (SUSAN, BILLY)
Whisky (SUSAN)
Cup of tea (INSPECTOR)
Piece of paper (MARY)
Pen, paper (LAWYER, SOCIAL WORKER)
Water, glass (LAWYER)

SOUND EFFECTS

TV cartoon
Gunshot
Music

NEW PLAYS

★ **INTIMATE APPAREL by Lynn Nottage.** The moving and lyrical story of a turn-of-the-century black seamstress whose gifted hands and sewing machine are the tools she uses to fashion her dreams from the whole cloth of her life's experiences. "…Nottage's play has a delicacy and eloquence that seem absolutely right for the time she is depicting…" *–NY Daily News.* "…thoughtful, affecting…The play offers poignant commentary on an era when the cut and color of one's dress—and of course, skin—determined whom one could and could not marry, sleep with, even talk to in public." *–Variety.* [2M, 4W] ISBN: 0-8222-2009-1

★ **BROOKLYN BOY by Donald Margulies.** A witty and insightful look at what happens to a writer when his novel hits the bestseller list. "The characters are beautifully drawn, the dialogue sparkles…" *–nytheatre.com.* "Few playwrights have the mastery to smartly investigate so much through a laugh-out-loud comedy that combines the vintage subject matter of successful writer-returning-to-ethnic-roots with the familiar mid-life crisis." *–Show Business Weekly.* [4M, 3W] ISBN: 0-8222-2074-1

★ **CROWNS by Regina Taylor.** Hats become a springboard for an exploration of black history and identity in this celebratory musical play. "Taylor pulls off a Hat Trick: She scores thrice, turning CROWNS into an artful amalgamation of oral history, fashion show, and musical theater…" *–TheatreMania.com.* "…wholly theatrical…Ms. Taylor has created a show that seems to arise out of spontaneous combustion, as if a bevy of department-store customers simultaneously decided to stage a revival meeting in the changing room." *–NY Times.* [1M, 6W (2 musicians)] ISBN: 0-8222-1963-8

★ **EXITS AND ENTRANCES by Athol Fugard.** The story of a relationship between a young playwright on the threshold of his career and an aging actor who has reached the end of his. "[Fugard] can say more with a single line than most playwrights convey in an entire script…Paraphrasing the title, it's safe to say this drama, making its memorable entrance into our consciousness, is unlikely to exit as long as a theater exists for exceptional work." *–Variety.* "A thought-provoking, elegant and engrossing new play…" *–Hollywood Reporter.* [2M] ISBN: 0-8222-2041-5

★ **BUG by Tracy Letts.** A thriller featuring a pair of star-crossed lovers in an Oklahoma City motel facing a bug invasion, paranoia, conspiracy theories and twisted psychological motives. "…obscenely exciting…top-flight craftsmanship. Buckle up and brace yourself…" *–NY Times.* "…[a] thoroughly outrageous and thoroughly entertaining play…the possibility of enemies, real and imagined, to squash has never been more theatrical." *–A.P.* [3M, 2W] ISBN: 0-8222-2016-4

★ **THOM PAIN (BASED ON NOTHING) by Will Eno.** An ordinary man muses on childhood, yearning, disappointment and loss, as he draws the audience into his last-ditch plea for empathy and enlightenment. "It's one of those treasured nights in the theater—treasured nights anywhere, for that matter—that can leave you both breathless with exhilaration and…in a puddle of tears." *–NY Times.* "Eno's words…are familiar, but proffered in a way that is constantly contradictory to our expectations. Beckett is certainly among his literary ancestors." *–nytheatre.com.* [1M] ISBN: 0-8222-2076-8

★ **THE LONG CHRISTMAS RIDE HOME by Paula Vogel.** Past, present and future collide on a snowy Christmas Eve for a troubled family of five. "…[a] lovely and hauntingly original family drama…a work that breathes so much life into the theater." *–Time Out.* "…[a] delicate visual feast…" *–NY Times.* "…brutal and lovely…the overall effect is magical." *–NY Newsday.* [3M, 3W] ISBN: 0-8222-2003-2

DRAMATISTS PLAY SERVICE, INC.
440 Park Avenue South, New York, NY 10016 212-683-8960 Fax 212-213-1539
postmaster@dramatists.com www.dramatists.com